God Thoughts

A Selection of Poems

SHIRLEY WIGLEY

Walton Publishing House
www.waltonpublishinghouse.com
Houston, Texas

Victorious Living Publishing
www.victoriouslivingfoundation.com
Philipsburg, St. Maarten

Printed in the United States of America

Library of Congress Cataloging in-Publication Data under ISBN herein.

ISBN# 978-1-953993-55-7 (Paperback)

Dedication

I dedicate *God Thoughts* to my daughter Juliette & grandson Khajeel.

May you always remember that:

"Through wisdom a house is built

And by understanding it is established.

By knowledge the rooms are filled

With all precious and pleasant riches."

Proverbs 24:3-4

Acknowledgements

Special thanks to God my Father for this wonderful gift he has given to me.

I gratefully acknowledge my daughter Juliette for giving me her support in the difficult times. May the good Lord bless you and keep you, and may you find strength to continue on.

To Mrs. Annette Lake for her advice and encouragement, and for being there for me to help make this book a reality.

To my brother and sisters for contributing to my dream.

To my sisters and brothers of the Christian Fellowship Church for your prayers and encouragement.

Thanks to you all.

Introduction

A Message From the Author

God Thoughts, the name of my book, is a selection of poems from my heart to your heart. I pray these poems will capture your soul, mind, and body.

Poetry is not just an expression, but what lies deep within your spirit. *God Thoughts* are His inspiring words. I pray that my poems will bring much freshness to your soul.

The late Dr. Myles Munroe once said, "The richest place on earth is not the sea, nor the banks. The richest place on earth is the burial ground, because there are people who died with books that have never been written, songs that have never been sung, houses that have never been built, pictures that have never been painted."

Do not let these rich resources die inside of you. What you are carrying, your generation needs it. What you have is not yours. Stir up the gift that is within you!

Thanks to all who made this dream of bringing *God Thoughts* into print, a reality.

The Thoughts Of God

The thoughts of God

As you can see

Are in these pages.

As you read you will understand

Why I call this book

God Thoughts.

Contents

❧

God Thoughts

If God's thoughts are not your thoughts

And his ways are not your ways

Then where are your thoughts

And where are your ways?

Are your thoughts the thoughts of evil men

And your ways, the ways of the world?

Let's not sit here idly thinking

What the world has to offer.

The world gives trouble and sin

But God gives life to win.

Let God's thoughts be your thoughts

And his ways your ways.

So think of the heavenly things

And not the earthly things.

...continued

The heavenly things are pure, holy, and rich.

You do not pay one cent for them.

The earthly things are costly.

You've got to spend a lot for them.

You're never satisfied, and you're never filled.

You always want more

And you're never sure.

So let the heavenly things be your desire

And earthly things you will not admire.

A Prisoner Of Sin

I was once a prisoner of sin;

In my heart, no peace.

Jesus came and rescued me;

Praise the Lord I am free!

So marred was my life;

not fit for any use.

But the potter who made this clay

Reached down and lifted me.

The patience he took with me,

To roll and make me,

To shape and fashion me,

He will do to you as he did with me.

If your life is marred

And seems no good,

Come to Jesus he will take your load.

A beautiful vessel your life will be

If Jesus Christ works in thee.

A Special Lady

S. Such a time like this you are dear to my heart.

P. Precious are your words that cannot depart.

E. Each time I listen you are cooing like a dove,

C. Caring for those who are poor and dismayed.

I. In your heart is a priceless love

A. Adorable like your Father who lives above.

L. Love flows from your heart, your children, and others;

L. Like any lady you are wonderful

A. Attractive, generous and true

D. Dedicated in everything you do

Y. Yes you are special.

A Wonderful Lady

A Mother is a wonderful person
She is a darling to have around
When you need understanding
She is the best friend that can be found.
She is someone you can count on for help
And encouragement too,
A Mother is a wonderful person
If she is a Mother like you.
Mother on this your special day,
We your children have this to say:
"We wish you God's love and blessings
On this the Second Sunday of May."

All Nations

All nations will come to your light.

Mighty men will see

The beauty of God's splendor

Radiating through us.

Foreigners will build your cities

Presidents will send you aid.

Though I destroyed you in my anger

I will have mercy through my grace.

Your eyes will shine with joy

Your heart will thrill,

Your tongue will tell

Of his providential will.

Angry

Have you ever been angry
And wished you had not uttered a word,
And it seemed that you were caught in space
And wondering how you got there?
The temperature dropped a while
Coming through thin air,
Then you remembered you had been angry
And never took control.
It has already gone forth
And can never return.
Ask forgiveness of sin;
For joy and peace to dwell within.
Then you will be free.
Always remember this
If you at any time become angry.

An Overwhelmed Heart

When your heart is overwhelmed
To whom will you turn?
Go to the Rock.
He is your strength and power;
He is your high tower.
Hold on to him.

When your heart is overwhelmed
To whom will you turn?
Run to the Rock.
He has been a shelter for us;
A strong tower from the enemy.
Love Him.

…continued

When your heart is overwhelmed

To whom will you turn?

Stand on the Rock.

He is your solid foundation.

He is your salvation.

Serve him!

Any Doubt In Your Mind?

———— ✦ ————

Have you any doubts in your mind
That seem to press you down?
Then give them to Jesus
Our great healer.

Have you any doubt in your mind?
Come unto him all ye that labor
Because in him you find rest.
Put him to the test,
He will fix it for you.

Have you any doubt in your mind?
Cease not to pray.
The answer may be long
But victory will come.
Wait on him I say.

A Race To Be Won

Have you begun to run the race

God called you to do?

Have your steps been bright along the way

Or have you backed out and gone astray?

This is no time to play the fool.

It is time to move on to the realms above.

Hasten on, it is almost midnight.

Let us turn from the wrong and do the right.

It is right to serve the Lord.

It is right to be in one accord.

Be frank with yourself.

Let the truth come forth.

Arise My People!

Arise my people!
Let your light shine!
For the glory of the Lord
Is pouring down.

Arise my people!
Jesus is near.
Put on your righteous garment
And occupy until he comes.

Arise my people!
Come together as one!
Let us unite
With God's only Son.

A Journey I Have Started

I have started on this journey

And I want to reach my goal.

At times my feet would hurt

And want to turn off the road.

I hear a voice say

"There is a cross to bear

And a crown to be won.

Press on my child, press on.

It is not a bed of roses.

You must pursue;

Get all the blessings

God has in store for you.

Never look back, look to the cross.

Keep your eyes on Jesus

You cannot be lost."

Be Wise

Be like the ants and be wise.

You will not understand

Why people come into our lives.

Think of the many things that happen to you.

Many times you were cast aside.

Many times you felt like giving up.

Then you realize life must go on.

So why bow your head in the sand

And feel life is not worth living?

See yourself as that woman

Who is not foolish, but wise.

Be Strong In The Lord

We are called to the battle field
To fight courageously.
No idling, no gossiping,
Only equipped with the Gospel.
This field calls for the strong ones
To lift the heavy burdens,
The broken homes, the troubled lives,
The many who are paralyzed.
In the power of his might,
Be strong!
Put on the armor of God
And having done this, stand!

Be Yourself

Father, never run away from your troubles.

Face each day with a smile.

Though the trials of this moment seem hard,

Soon they will fly away.

Rise from your sleep.

Hear the birds and the bees.

Hear the wind whistling through the trees.

Hear the bells ringing

And the choirs singing.

Father arise! Arise!

Be yourself and not another.

Have a vision and face the future.

Have wisdom and understanding.

Think on these words.

Lay them on your heart.

Building The House

As I watch the house
Our Lord is building,
It is a beautiful work of art.
As it takes shape and style
Its beauty is beyond the natural eyes.
Its materials are rich in color;
They are more valuable than gold.
And as you pass and see the sign
It has been purchased with His blood.
If your life is made of one of these materials
Gold, silver, or precious stone,
It will be tried with fire
And your identity will be known.
Yes, God has called us to build together,
Not just a certain part.

…continued

Togetherness brings unity

And the work has just started.

So build your life on the Lord Jesus Christ.

Build your life on Him today.

You are His material.

Come, let Him use you.

Choose Now

Someday you say I will seek the Lord.

Someday I will make my choice.

Someday, someday, I will take heed of his words

And answer the Spirit's voice.

God's time is now, for the days fly fast

And swiftly the seasons roll.

Today is yours, it may be the last,

Choose life for your priceless soul.

Choose now, for a soul is at stake.

Oh! What will your answer be?

It is life or death,

And the choice you make is made for eternity.

Choose now for the Lord is here.

For you He patiently waits.

Choose now while the call is clear;

Tomorrow may be too late.

Christ Is The Christ For All Crises

When the storm in your life is raging
And you are feeling low,
Don't give up, saying I am through
There is one who can fix it for you.
He is the Christ for all crises.
When your marriage is on the rocks
And everything has tumbled down,
Build your life on him.
He is the master of all conditions.
Let the storms rage
And the winds blow,
For Christ is the Christ in your crisis.
Crisis comes one way or the other.
It is one thing we cannot avoid altogether.
In spite of the pressure,
Let the Almighty God be in control.
Let Christ be the Christ in your crisis.

Come And Drink

Are you thirsty, come and drink.

If you have no money

Come, take your choice of wine and milk.

Why spend your money on food that gives no strength?

Listen, and I'll tell you

Where to get good food for the soul.

You have to seek the Lord while He can be found;

Call upon Him while He is near.

Let men cast off their wicked deeds,

Let them banish from their minds

The very thoughts of doing wrong

And turn to the Lord

That He may have mercy upon them.

Seek our God, for He will abundantly pardon.

Congratulations!

Congratulations!

Happy Anniversary

On this your first year of victory.

God bless you and your host

On this day you treasure most.

I know you worked very hard

To make this anniversary a success.

The song of praise, the joy of love

Each word is sealed above.

Continue to do the work of God

Which may not be easy at times.

But with God in the vessel,

You can smile at the storm.

Oh! Give thanks unto God for He is good.

Depending on His Holy name,

The redeemed of the Lord should sing

Hallelujah, to the King.

Congrats

Congrats to you graduates

You have sat your test

By doing your best.

You have passed

But this is not the last.

It is just the beginning of your achievement.

There is more to explore

If you just open the door.

Set your goal, and go after it.

Don't give up, saying, I'll quit.

That dream you have dreamt

You must achieve it;

Begin to see it.

Tell yourself I will make it.

Do not misuse and abuse it.

…continued

The choice you make will be your destiny.

What you have started, you are able to finish.

Never settle for less.

You must strive for the best.

You must strive for excellence!

Deliverance

The three Hebrew boys answered:

"O King Nebuchadnezzar

We have no need to answer you in this matter;

Our God whom we serve is able to deliver us.

O King to your golden image we will not bow.

We care not when, where, or why.

Fiery furnace is no trouble at all;

The God of our Father will not let us fall."

Did not we cast three men in the fire?

I am confused, said the King.

Get me higher!

There is another, making four.

The fourth is the Son of God.

Zeal and determination we should have.

We must fight with all our might.

The three Hebrew boys they did not resist

They had one desire, to go through the test.

We Enthrone You Lord

O God enthroned in heaven,
We lift our eyes to you.
The Lord Jehovah,
Our King Messiah,
Who lives and reigns forever.

O God enthroned in heaven,
We lift our hands to you
In worship and in praise,
For you are our Savior;
You are our Redeemer;
The Omnipotent One.

O God enthroned in heaven,
We lift our voices to you
In spirit and in truth.
With one heart
We bow and adore thee
Our Sovereign King
The Almighty.

Fear Not

My light and my salvation is from the Lord;

He protects me from danger.

When evil men come to destroy me

They will stumble and fall.

Though ten thousands march against me

My heart shall not fear

For my confidence is in the Lord.

One thing is my desire:

Living in the presence of my Lord.

When troubles come, in Him I will hide

Out of the reach of my enemies.

Praises of sacrifice and thanksgiving

I will offer unto Him.

Fishers Of Men

F. Faithful you must be

I. In this troubled time.

S. Souls are dying; need to be saved.

H. Hasten on my brothers;

E. Each one has a task to do.

R. Rise up and take your stand,

S. Sow the word the best way you can.

O. Over and over you have heard the call.

F. Faint and weary you have become.

M. Men of God take him at His word.

E. Enter in the joy of the Lord

N. Never to lose sight again.

Father And His Son

Father when was the last time

You cuddled your son in your arms

And said, I love you?

When was the last time

You took your son for a drive

And shared with him

A few of the things that happened in your life?

When was the last time

You had a game of domino or cricket

And shared with him

That in this life he can make it?

The son you train today

Will be the Father tomorrow.

Show your son you care

From now, till the rest of your years.

…continued

Teach your son the word of God.

Teach him to pray;

Teach him to trust in God

Morning, noon, and night.

Father, love your son.

Stop calling him foolish names,

For that seed you sow today

You will reap tomorrow.

Do not tell your son

He won't become anything.

You see, God built into your son

Such beautiful abilities.

God knew what your son would be.

If he is not doing well,

Try and help him.

Continue to instill in your son

The things he will appreciate.

The relationship between you and your son

Will determine his destiny.

God's People

Tell me what is wrong with God's people.

His only Son he gave

Shed his life blood

That you and I can be saved.

Tell me what is wrong with God's people?

Through the barren land they came

Shouting "Moses, water!"

Their thirsty souls were filled.

Tell me what is wrong with God's people?

He promised He will not leave us,

Nothing shall over take us

If we only believe.

...continued

We as God's people, tell me what is wrong?

Isn't He a God to his word?

Isn't He a God who never fails?

Then why are we so troubled;

So bitter in soul?

Cast your burden on Him

He is in control.

The Thoughts Of God

God's thoughts can be seen
And heard in the wind.
They can be seen in the life of men.
You can see them as you walk
Along the seashore.
You can see them in the faces
Of our little boys and girls.
God's thoughts are unique.
You must express them.
You got to tell them
To everyone far and near.
The thoughts of God
Are His inspired word.

Go And Tell

Go, Tell someone that Jesus is Lord
Tell them he died to save us all.
He gave his life on that cruel tree
So you and I can be free.

Go tell someone He is mighty to save.
Tell them the choice is yours.
Choose Jesus He is a wonderful friend
Tell them He is coming again.

Go feed the hungry
With the true bread of life.
Give them a cup of cold water
And their thirsty souls will be satisfied.

Go, tell someone who is hurting within,
Tell them the remedy is to be free from sin.
Accept him by faith is the only way,
Today is your day.

Good Morning Holy Spirit

Good morning Holy Spirit,
How are you today?
With that still small voice
He reassures me everything is okay.

Good morning Holy Spirit.
Just to know you,
I come humbly kneeling
Prostrate at your feet.

Good morning Holy Spirit
Speak through me today;
I can feel your presence
In the night and the day.

Good morning Holy Spirit
You are always near;
I will not be afraid
Because you are always there.

Great Faith

Consider the lilies,
They neither toil nor spin
Yet still our Father waters them.
He wonderfully cares for the flowers
He truly cares for you.

Faith that can move mountains,
Faith that can fill fountains,
Little faith I cannot attain
Great faith I must regain.

Faith in God as you can see
Mountain-moving is sure to be.
Doubt not in your heart
But believe in every part.

…continued

When you pray, have faith for the answer.

Doubt fills your heart saying it is cancer.

Doctors give you up, we can do no more.

Faith says; run to Jesus, He has the cure.

Give Thanks

Let us bow and give praise to the Master.

Thank Him for delivering us from many disasters.

Let us lift our hearts and sing;

Let us give honor to our King.

Give Him thanks for this hour.

Thank Him for today.

Put Him on your list

He is the first, He is the best.

Between us His covenant was made.

He said, remind Him of His words.

Heaven and earth will proclaim

The glory of His name.

Let us forget the petty things.

To us His salvation brings.

Accept the love He offers you,

...continued

He knows what is best for you.

Let everyone know He is your Lord.

There are many who have never heard.

Tell them He is mighty to save.

Tell them He is coming again.

Humility

The attitude of humility,

Multiply by grace.

The substance of it is unity

In it you will find your place.

Shift away carnality,

Then add a little love.

For at the heart of love,

is true humility.

In Your Presence

Lord, as I kneel in your presence,

You are the Holy One;

You are the Almighty.

With a repentant heart I come.

Remove my sins away

And I shall be clean.

Lord, as I kneel in your presence,

I am not the child

I want to be,

But you have chosen me.

You have set me free.

Praise your wonderful name.

I Am Happy

You ask me why I am happy,
I will tell you why.
My life has been transformed
Through the blood of the Lamb.
Jesus paid it there for me
On the cross of Calvary.
He paid once and for all
That I can heed the call.

How Can We Take It Easy?

How can we take it easy

When many are plunging in sin?

How can we take it easy?

Many are dying within.

How can we take it easy?

Our world is upside down.

How can we take it easy?

He said to preach the word.

How can we take it easy?

Our streets are full of gangs.

How can we take it easy?

We must extend a helping hand.

I Will Rejoice In The Lord

Although the fig tree shall not blossom,

Nor fruit the vine shall yield,

The labor of the olive fails

And barren be the field,

Though cut off from the fold,

Yet, I will rejoice in God my Lord

My strength, my help, my all.

I Love You

One and One is Two,

Jesus, I love you.

Two and Two is Four,

Thank you for knocking at my door.

Three and Three is Six

You deliver me from Satan's tricks.

Four and Four is Eight,

Help me not to be late.

Five and Five is Ten,

On you I must depend.

Six and Six is Twelve,

Because of your blood

I can live.

It Shall Come To Pass

We are living in troubled times
Crucial days are here.
Lift up your head my people
He is nearer than you think.
Famine, pestilence on every hand,
Cries of our children through the land.
Fathers are sighing,
Mothers are travailing
Because of the things coming up on us.
Be not terrified
Of the things you are hearing;
They must come to pass.
So trim your lamps,
Let them be burning
For it is almost midnight.

I Will Follow You All The Way

Lord I need you to be as my guard;
I need you to be at my side.
Each step in the day,
I will follow you all the way.

Sometimes it is rough;
Sometimes the way seems tough.
If I put you to the test,
I am sure I will be at rest.
I will follow you all the way.

Many testify of you,
Many turn their backs on you,
But Father I will be true;
I will follow you all the way.

Is There Room In Your Heart?

Is there room in your heart

For the Savior today?

Think of how they mocked Him

As He hung there on the tree.

Great drops of blood

Flowed from His brow;

In His hands, His feet, the nails were driven.

Through His side the sword was pierced.

Vinegar mingled with gall was His drink;

They spat on Him;

They took the reed

And smote on the head.

He gave up the ghost.

… continued

But one thing I know,

The grave was not His home.

He arose Triumphantly!

There was no room in the inn.

Is there room in your heart for Him?

In Time Of Storm

In times of storm, you can be calm.
In times of strife, there is no alarm.
Fight the battle not by yourself,
The battle is the Lord's.

When trouble strikes, fear not.
The one who is bigger than your problems,
He's never lost a battle nor a case.
Put your trust in Him, He is never late.

He is your refuge, He is your strength.
He is your rock on Him you will depend
Casting your burden on Him, He will not fail.
He is your deliverer, your all in all.

... continued

Brethren, put your trust in Him

And not in the flesh.

He is strong and powerful

Cling to him every day,

He is safe and secure.

Just Believe In Yourself

If you know who you are

And where you are going

It makes a big difference.

Look not at what men may think

Regardless of the circumstances

And the consequences.

If you know who you are

And where you are going

You can make it.

Jesus Did It For Me

I wonder at times where I would be
If Jesus did not die for me.
Like a lost sheep out in the cold
I'd live in sin and agony.
Out of the depths I cried
And Jesus heard my sinful plea.
My sins are gone and my heart is now free.
Praise God I am secure in Him.
At times I feel like the stone
That was rejected and cast aside.
But when I think of Jesus
I say in Him I will abide.
I look up and see His face,
I am chosen and saved by grace.

Jesus Is Alive

Jesus is alive,

The stone has been rolled away.

He is alive;

He is no longer where He lay.

He is alive;

I can hear the angel say:

"Let us rejoice today

For Jesus is Alive."

He is alive!

Five thousand souls were fed

With two fish and five loaves of bread.

He is alive!

Come see a man who told me all I ever did;

Jesus is alive!

…continued

The woman with the issue of blood

She touched the hem of His garment

And her fountain of blood ended.

He is alive! Jesus is alive!

He is alive, our sins have been forgiven.

He is alive; the only way to heaven.

Accept him today, for Jesus is alive!

Jonah

God told Jonah,

Come, go to Nineveh.

In forty days

I will destroy her.

Jonah heard the word

And turned away from God.

He bought his ticket

And found himself in Tarshish.

He got on board

And hid himself from the Lord.

But as the ship sailed along,

Suddenly, there was a terrible storm.

Fearing for their lives,

The sailors shouted to their god

And threw their cargo overboard

…continued

While Jonah lay asleep in the hull.

What shall we do to stop the storm?

Throw me overboard, and the sea will be calm.

Then Jonah prayed inside the fish,

Lord, why did I not resist?

When hope was gone

I turned my thoughts to the Lord.

How can I thank you for all you have done?

The Lord ordered the fish

To spit up Jonah on the beach.

Jonah cried, "Lord, what a release."

He obeyed and went to Nineveh

The people bowed their knees and surrendered.

God saw that they stopped sinning.

He said to Jonah, that is preaching.

Like Jonah, we have come short

We can learn a lesson;

Repent!

Jesus Is The Light Of The World

As I walk this road of life
It seems like no one cares.
But up ahead, I hear a voice,
"I am Jesus, the light of the world."

You do not have to lay in the mire
Nor in the dust of the ground,
Arise, take your stand
For Jesus is the light of the world.

The astrologers are not the light,
Neither the magician nor the psychic.
The true and only light
Is no other, but the Lord Jesus Christ.

…continued

So do not turn your back on Him my friends.

Open your heart today,

Accept him now, before it is too late

For Jesus is the true light and the way.

Keep On Going!

You have been persecuted all your life.

You have been through much strife.

Brethren I am encouraging you

Even though the seas are raging high,

Keep on! Keep on going!

We know that many obstacles will be in your way.

We know it's not easy in this day.

Let your anchor down, and your sail fly high;

Keep on! Keep on going!

Get in the secret place with God

Then you will not be molested on the road.

That secret place is prayer,

You can do that anywhere.

Keep on! Keep on going!

...continued

Brethren be like the eagle,

Spread your wings and fly high.

The storms of life are not easy.

But let your feet be like hind's feet.

Holding fast to the rock

That is higher than you and I,

Keep on! Keep on going!

Let Not Your Heart Be Troubled

Why should your heart be troubled?

Why should you fear?

Our God is Almighty

He truly cares.

Why should your heart be troubled?

God is on our side.

Take him at His word.

In Him, we shall abide.

Why should your heart be troubled?

Jesus is the truth, the life, the way.

He has gone to prepare a mansion for

our homecoming day.

...continued

Why should your heart be troubled?

Lift your spirit high.

Take courage my brothers and sisters,

Our redemption draweth nigh.

Let Us Go Forth To Conquer

God has raised a new breed of people
To go in and possess the land.
You must have Joshua and Caleb spirits.
Through God's power we will stand.

Nations must be conquered.
The isles of the sea
His territories shall be taken;
And we shall spoil the enemy.

Going around Jericho
It was seven times.
The people made one shout
And the walls came tumbling down.

...continued

Together in this battle
We all shall fight.
Victory shall be ours
When we all unite.

Let Your Glory Fill The Earth

O Lord, you have taught us

To praise you perfectly.

May our examples shame

And silence the enemy.

O Lord, our God

The majesty and glory of your name,

Fill all the earth.

Let all voices be heard

Loud and clear

To glorify your precious name.

With one voice we will sing

Praise to our Heavenly King.

O Lord, our God,

The majesty and glory of your name,

Fill all the earth.

Living Water

The well of mercy is ever flowing.
Flowing for you and me.
Come drink from the springs of mercy
Flowing so full and free.

Are you thirsty, are you weary?
Drink from this living water,
Free for asking and receiving
Only yield to the Master.

The woman of Samaria finds
This water was purified
Asking for a drink, she was filled
With the living water from the well.

…continued

Welcome to this spring.
Always refreshing;
Accept the offer.
You will never regret
Using this living water.

My Shepherd

The Lord is my shepherd
What more could I ask?
He has given me every promise
From His Holy book.
A table before me, He furnished
In the presence of my foes;
By still waters He leads,
My cup He overflows.
My head He with oil anoints
So I can stand with power.
My dwelling place shall ever be
Within His house forever.

Mother's Prayer

On a clear morning I awoke from sleep,

I heard Mother praying

With a trembling voice:

"Lord bless my daughter

Make her your choice."

She prayed from ten minutes to one hour.

I shook my head, and said, O what a Mother,

Isn't she wonderful? What a lady.

She takes time to be in prayer.

She reads her Bible as often as can be

From the creation to the Holy City;

Each line she measures, each verse she treasures

From the book of books, the Bible.

She rose from her knees with a pleasant smile.

Her prayer has been answered.

Lord, thank you for a Mother

Who is gentle, meek, and mild.

Mother

Mother, you are our pillow

On which we lay our heads.

Yes, you were our comfort

When no one else was there.

You were our source of strength

When others put us down.

You are a builder, and forever building.

You are a fighter, and always achieving.

Because all these you have done,

We join and say

Happy Mother's Day.

Mama I Love You

Mama, you are wonderful and kind
You are always on my mind.
For the things you have done,
Mama, I love you.

Mama, I remember the times
When no food was there
You knelt at your bedside
And God answered your prayer.
Mama, I love you.

Mama, I remember when we were sick
You were the only mechanic.
You lay your hands on the broken part.
Mama, I love you.

…continued

Mama, I know someday
You have to part.
Mama, I know it will break my heart.
Mama, I love you.

My Love

Mother, I am giving you my love;
A love like the dew drops from above.
A love you must regain,
Mother, this love must remain.

Mother, I am sending you my love.
A love you cannot count;
A love you will not doubt.
A love which is more than a life time's worth
Mother, you are dear to my heart.

Mother, I am throwing you my love.
A love you will not regret.
A love that cannot fail;
A love you will appreciate.
Mother, you are loved.

...continued

Mother, I am loving you with my love.

A love that is precious and bright;

A love that has great insight;

A love that is always right.

Mother, you are my delight.

My Little Gift

I may not have a gift for you Father,

But I have a simple prayer.

Lord bless my Father,

Make him your own.

I may not have a gift but a little song,

The melody is sweetly ringing.

The words of it are soft and sweet

Father, your love we appreciate.

This little rose from Mama's garden,

Father, take this, use it.

The memory of it

You will never forget.

Though simple it is a token of our love.

The services you rendered are sealed above.

…continued

Out of our hearts we say, thank you
For the faithfulness of our Father.

One Minute

I have only one minute;

Only sixty seconds in it;

Forced upon me, cannot refuse it.

Did not seek it, did not choose it;

But it is up to me to use it.

I will suffer if I lose it.

Give account if I abuse it.

It is only just a minute

But eternity is in it.

No More In A Manger

He is no more in a manger
Nor in the cattle stall.
He is at the Father's right hand
Interceding for all.

He is no more in a manger
He has risen from the dead.
He has redeemed us from sin
That you and I can live.

He is no more in a manger
He has taken our place,
So we can enter into His presence
By His saving grace.

...continued

He is no more in a manger

He is coming again.

He is not coming as a Judge

But as King of all Kings.

Only Your Best Is Good Enough

As I sat in my class room
On the day of my test,
The voice of my teacher echoed:
"Only your best is good enough!"
As I thought on the subjects
Math, English, Dutch and Spanish,
I asked myself, "What is my best?"
The most I could do was my reply.
The best subjects I truly fail,
Math and English are the best of all.
So if you have sat your test
And you have failed
Get up from there and try again.
For when you have done your best
And no more to be done,
You can say like your teacher:
"Only my best is surely good enough."

Pre-Anointed For The Battle

Pre-anointed for the battle
Hear the soldiers marching on.
Arm yourself; as dangerous
is the time in which we are living.

Pre-anointed for the battle
In his hands he took five stones.
You come to me with shield and sword
But I come to you in the name of the Lord.

Pre-anointed for the battle
Hear the shouting in the camp.
David has slain Goliath
And Israel has triumphed.

...continued

Pre-anointed for the battle

Lift your head, stand strong.

Jesus the conquering Lion

Fought the battle

And won the war.

Pray

In times like these we need to pray.

When things are dark and dreary;

When you don't feel like praying, pray.

When your friends talk about you

When they drag your name to the ground

Even when you don't feel like turning around, pray.

When your children do not obey you

Even when they have fallen through

Do not take on what they do, just pray.

When you go to sleep at night

When you awake through the night

When you go through the day

Even when you are on the highway, pray.

Do not get upset when things do not work out.

Even when you become the laughing stock of everyone;

…continued

When you are feeling uptight

When things are not looking bright

Whether you are wrong or right, just pray.

When your children take everything for granted

Do not frown or fret.

Let them know they will regret, just pray.

When all around is crumbling down

Stand firm in Jesus.

When you have come to the end

And you hear well done my friend

Then you will say:

"Thank God I have prayed."

Salvation To Everyone

You have heard of salvation

Through sermons and songs.

Why don't you accept Him?

You know what you are doing is wrong.

You may put it off until tomorrow or next year.

To accept Him now is far better

Than wait until it is too late.

You may say in your heart

I will have my pleasure and my fling.

Accept Him now while the Spirit is wooing.

In a twinkling of an eye Jesus will be here;

You can feel His presence in the air

So take Him as your Savior today.

Sowing Seeds

Take a look into my garden
And you will find the names of seeds.
You will find the seed of love;
It is tall and green
It reaches to the throne above.

In this part of my garden
Is the seed of kindness;
It is very wide
It can master any tide.

Along this row
You will find the seed of humility.
It burns deep down;
It can fit any crown.

...continued

At this end of my garden

Is the seed of patience.

It is very cool

It is always springing.

Time

Spending time with your children

Is the best gift you can give.

Money and toys cannot satisfy

The emptiness within.

Time to hear their aches and pain

For time lost cannot be regained.

Time to communicate;

Time to appreciate

The good things they have done.

If you do not spend time with your children

Drugs and television will be their friends

And they will have a bitter end.

Do not spend all your time making money.

Five minutes is just right.

Time spent with your children

Is the best medicine on earth.

Time

Time is important, buy it.

Time is free, love it.

Time is right, say it.

Time is short, use it.

Thank You Mother

Times change, so do men.

My Mother is a woman of all women.

She cooks, washes, and combs my hair.

I cannot find another so dear.

She spanks me when I am rude,

She rewards me when I am good.

She takes time to teach me to pray.

In prayer I have learned the golden rule.

Now I am grown and on my own,

I still can recall the things I have learned.

Thank you Mother for teaching me these things.

They cause me to know

That life is worth living.

The Leper

Lord, I know I am a leper
But I need you more than ever.
Society has isolated me
But Lord you love me.
The leper came and worshiped Him.
Lord, if it is your will
You can make me clean.
He stretched out His hand
And touched the man.
Immediately his leprosy was gone.
Our sin, sick souls are like the leper
Who needed a touch from the Savior.
Come to Him, He will make you whole.

Trust Him

Trust Him with all your heart;

Trust Him if you are going to depart.

Trust Him in whatever you do,

Trust Him wherever you go.

Trust Him for what He has done.

Trust Him for sending His Son.

Trust Him because He loves you.

Trust Him for dying for you.

Trust Him when times are hard.

Trust Him your food He will provide.

Trust Him for this everyday;

Trust Him and always pray.

The Heavens Declare

The heavens declare
The glory of God.
They are a marvelous display
Of His craftsmanship.
Day and night they keep on
Telling about God
Without a sound or a word.
Silent in the sky,
Their message reaches out to the world.
The sun is in the heavens
Moving across the sky;
As radiant as a bridegroom
Going to his wedding.
As an athlete running a race,
From end to end the sun crosses the heavens;
And none can hide from its heat.

The Lamb

Behold the Lamb

With wings of snowy white.

He cometh with ten thousand saints

To judge the world with His might.

Behold the Lamb.

Glorious is He.

He cometh in the clouds

And every eye shall see.

The mockers and sorcerers

They too will see.

What joy and peace

To behold the Lamb

Who has redeemed us from sin

And sealed us with His love.

The Shaking Time

There is a shaking in the atmosphere;

It is here, there, and everywhere.

In governments, in schools, in our society;

Yes, right in our backyard.

Many hearts are failing with fear

Wondering if this great shaking

Will be in the coming year.

One thing I surely know

What God said He will do.

It will be a shaking;

It will come through.

The Church cannot be shaken.

On solid ground it stands.

Our peace cannot be shaken.

It cannot be disturbed by anyone.

The joy of the Lord is our strength.

The Year Of Jubilee

On the drugs of sin I was hooked.
Did not care of God nor his Son,
Yet he beckoned me come;
Salvation is for everyone.
The time of the Jubilee.

Total delivery is given to all
From hell's misery.
No more slave to sin.
Convinced of the peace within.
Year of Jubilee.

No time to mourn.
No time to groan.

…continued

The price of sin has been paid;
Liberated within.
Free from sin.
The song of Jubilee.

The time has come
The time is ripe
Friends, look at the eastern sky.
The clouds are lowering;
God's timing is at hand.
Freedom of Jubilee.

Do not turn your back
And walk away my friends.
Accept Him now;
It is never too late.
When He crowns you at the gate
It will be the change of Jubilee.

Wait On The Lord

Wait on the Lord you'll never go wrong.

Wait on the Lord you will be singing a song.

Take your time in life

Never run too fast.

Then you will shout the victory

Free, free, free at last!

Wait on the Lord, He is always true.

Wait on the Lord he will encourage you.

His word He will teach;

In a plain path you will reach.

Wait on the Lord, your strength He will renew.

Wait on the Lord His righteousness you pursue.

Keep your eyes on the road, never look back,

Then you will say, thank God I followed the track.

Why Complain?

Why complain when you have a meal to eat?

Why complain when you have shoes on your feet?

Why complain of the sunshine and the rain?

Why complain about harvest and grain?

Why complain when you can pray?

Why complain?

The answer is on the way.

Why complain of yesterday or today?

Why complain?

He is the truth, life, and the way.

Why complain when you can read the word?

Why complain when there are people
who have never heard?

Why complain when you've been accepted and
forgiven?

Why complain?

You are on your way to heaven.

We Shall Arise

When we fall we shall arise.

Regardless of who will criticize

We will surely get up

And shake off the dust.

Like the prodigal son

We have drifted far from home.

Not knowing Father was seeking for us

His children who were astray.

David too did arise.

He told us the reason:

"Lord, I have sinned and come short.

Take every sin and blot them out of my heart."

So when you have fallen and are in despair,

Take courage and get up.

Reach out by faith; hold His hands.

Jesus, the one who understands.

Woman Come Forth To Go Forth

God has called us to go forth

But too long we are at ease in Zion.

And we have hung our harp on the willow tree

Saying this is not for me.

Regardless who is not going,

We must take up the challenge.

He has given us the tools

To root out, pull down, pluck up, and to destroy.

Tighten your girdle of truth

And cry out.

As women, we must travail

Until we bring forth that man child.

This is not the time for intermission;

...continued

It is the time for intercession

For there is a message for the nations.

Yes, He is depending on us.

Is there someone he can trust?

Do not delay or go astray

Come forth, go forth, today.

You Are The Only One

You are the only one.

You are my only hope

Who paid the price For my sins.

God, I have been so wrong

For so long,

But today I put down my weapon

Of rebellion

And I accept you in humility.

Enough of my way;

And it is now your way

For the rest of my life.

And now Lord, I commit myself

Completely to you.

Your Armor

Take unto you the armor of God
So you can stand in this spirit world.
We do not fight things that are good
We fight those demonic powers.
Your loins must be girded
With the strong belt of truth.
Keep it tightened, it is your spiritual suit.
The breastplate of righteousness must be on
And fight in this battle the best way you can.
The shield of faith is your protection
Which will quench the fiery darts.
Your helmet of Salvation;
Your sword in hand
And having done all, you must stand.
As children of God we must not delay.
Do what you can while it is day.
Be that soldier who will fear no foe.
The price has been paid long, long ago.

You Soon Will Find

Each morning when you awake,
Just offer God the day;
Each task you undertake,
Whether work or play.
Offer him your happiness,
Your cares and troubles too.
Tell him that you won't forget
All he has done for you.
Now if you follow this recipe
You will surely soon find,
Your life is without care
And full of bright sunshine.

Your Heart

Mother your heart is like this rose bud

Blooming every hour.

The fragrance of this petal,

That unfolds after the shower.

As you separate each petal,

Let it remind you that if you are faithful,

You will be transformed like this petal

From this rough world

Into your heavenly home.

Each rose has its leaves and thorns.

In spite of the suffering in this hour,

God who can preserve this plant

Can preserve you from every misfortune.

Ah! Mother, a flower of the earth;

You are alive now but soon will fly away.

But in heaven, there awaits you Mother

Every blessing.

About The Author

Shirley Wigley was born on the Island of Nevis in a little village called Rawlins. She migrated to the Island of St. Maarten on the 28th of January 1971 where she began writing poetry in 1979. Wigley considers herself blessed to have such virtues locked on the inside, which she displays through her talent of poetry. She describes her poetry as hidden treasures that when found, light up your whole world. Some may ask, "Can any good thing come out of Nevis?" Wigley answers, "Yes!"

www.ingramcontent.com/pod-product-compliance
Lightning Source LLC
Chambersburg PA
CBHW071016120626
46546CB00003B/1115